SECOND EDITION

STRING QUARTET
SCORE AND PARTS
-VIOLIN
-VIOLIN
-VIOLA
-CELLO

I0620371

# 10 CHRISTMAS SONGS FOR STRING QUARTET

JEFF BRATZ

## HarmonyTabs

Sign up for the HarmonyTabs email list to keep up with new music releases, upcoming publications, and promotions:

HARMONYTABS EMAIL LIST

10 CHRISTMAS SONGS FOR STRING QUARTET
SECOND EDITION
Copyright © 2025 Jeff Bratz

To request permission, contact the publisher at publishing@HarmonyTabsMusic.com

ISBN: 978-1-961735-20-0 (paperback)
ISBN: 978-1-961735-21-7 (eBook)
ISMN: 979-0-60026-074-4 (paperback)
ISMN: 979-0-60026-075-1 (eBook)

First paperback edition October 2022

Printed in the United States of America

HarmonyTabs Music

HarmonyTabsMusic.com

# Contents

# INTRO

First, thank you for buying this songbook. I know there are a lot of options out there and I'm honored you landed here.

I hope these songs will be as fun for you to play through as they were for me to arrange. I've always loved the holiday season and I think that's largely due to the music that fills the air in every store, car, home, and everywhere else. I like to believe that in some small part this book will add to the spirit.

On the last page of the score and on each part is a QR code. That code will lead you to a homepage for that song where you can find additional resources including audio/video where you can hear the tune and find optional rehearsal tracks.

If at any point you have any questions, comments, suggestions, or anything else, please feel free to drop me a line: Jeff@HarmonyTabs.com.

Happy music-ing!
-Jeff

# ANGELS WE HAVE HEARD ON HIGH

Traditional French Carol
Arr. Jeff Bratz

AWHHOH (SQ)
11-11-24

# ANGELS WE HAVE HEARD ON HIGH

AWHHOH (SQ)
11-11-24

# ANGELS WE HAVE HEARD ON HIGH

Violin I

Traditional French Carol
Arr. Jeff Bratz

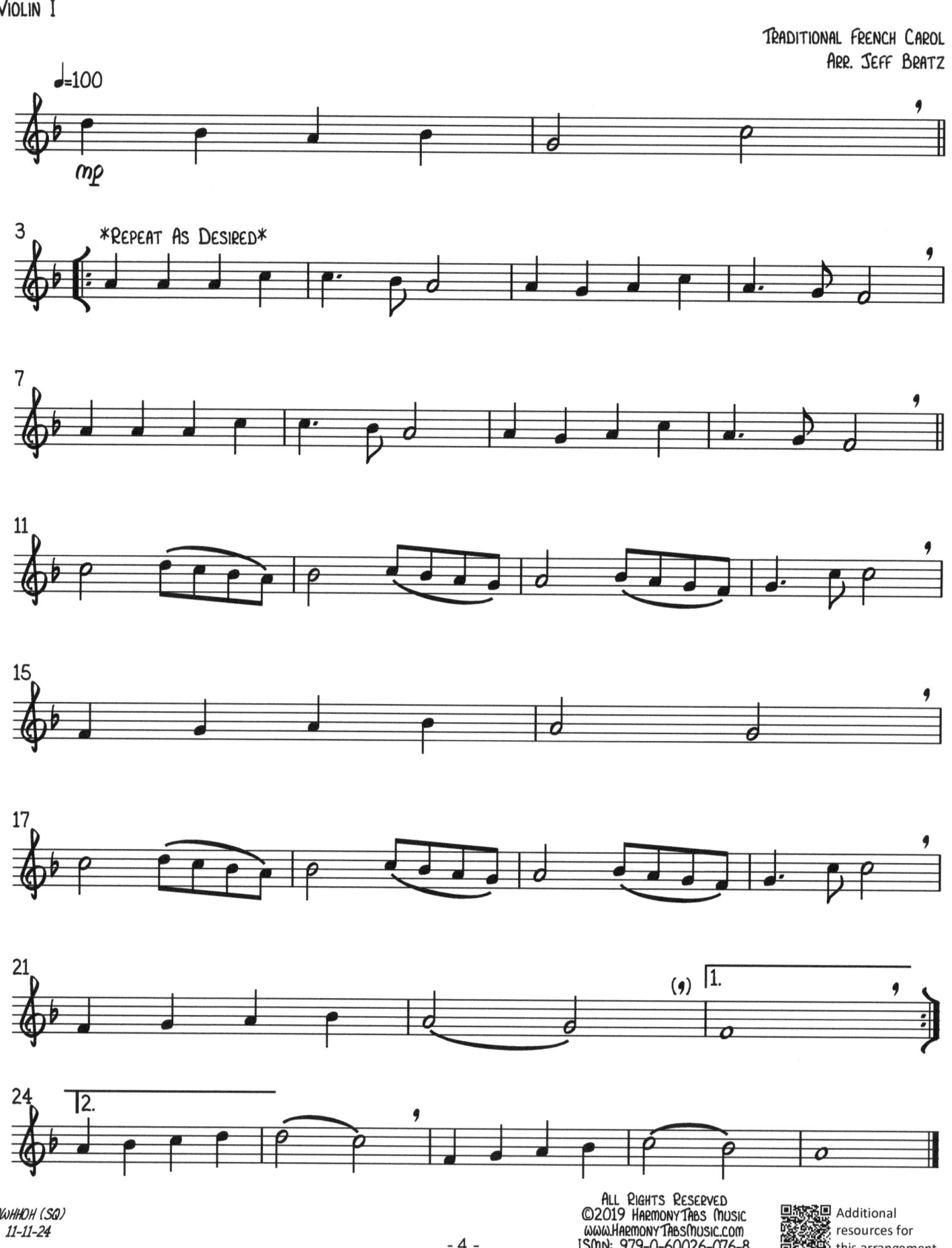

AWHHOH (SQ)
11-11-24
ISMN: 979-0-60026-076-8

Additional resources for this arrangement

- 4 -

# ANGELS WE HAVE HEARD ON HIGH

Violin II

Traditional French Carol
Arr. Jeff Bratz

Additional resources for this arrangement

AWHHOH (SQ)
11-11-24

# ANGELS WE HAVE HEARD ON HIGH

Viola

Traditional French Carol
Arr. Jeff Bratz

- 6 -

Additional resources for this arrangement

# ANGELS WE HAVE HEARD ON HIGH

Cello

Traditional French Carol
Arr. Jeff Bratz

Additional resources for this arrangement

- 7 -

AWHHOH (SQ)
11-11-24

# AULD LANG SYNE

Poem by Robert Burns
Arr. Jeff Bratz

ALS (SQ)
11-11-24

# AULD LANG SYNE

ALS (SQ)
11-11-24

# AULD LANG SYNE

Poem by Robert Burns
Arr. Jeff Bratz

ALS (SQ)
11-11-24

Additional resources for this arrangement

# AULD LANG SYNE

Poem by Robert Burns
Arr. Jeff Bratz

©2018 HarmonyTabs Music
www.HarmonyTabsMusic.com
ISMN: 979-0-60026-077-5

Additional resources for this arrangement

- 11 -

ALS (SQ)
11-11-24

# AULD LANG SYNE

Viola

Poem by Robert Burns
Arr. Jeff Bratz

ALS (SQ)
11-11-24

- 12 -

Additional resources for this arrangement

# AULD LANG SYNE

Cello

Poem by Robert Burns
Arr. Jeff Bratz

Additional resources for this arrangement

ALS (SQ)
11-11-24

# AWAY IN A MANGER

William J. Kirkpatrick
and James R. Murray
Arr. Jeff Bratz

AIAM (SQ)
11-15-24

- 14 -

# AWAY IN A MANGER

AIAM (SQ)
11-15-24

# AWAY IN A MANGER

AIAM (SQ)
11-15-24

# AWAY IN A MANGER

Violin I

William J. Kirkpatrick
and James R. Murray
Arr. Jeff Bratz

AIAM (SQ)
11-15-24

- 18 -

Additional resources for this arrangement

# AWAY IN A MANGER

William J. Kirkpatrick
and James R. Murray
Arr. Jeff Bratz

Violin II

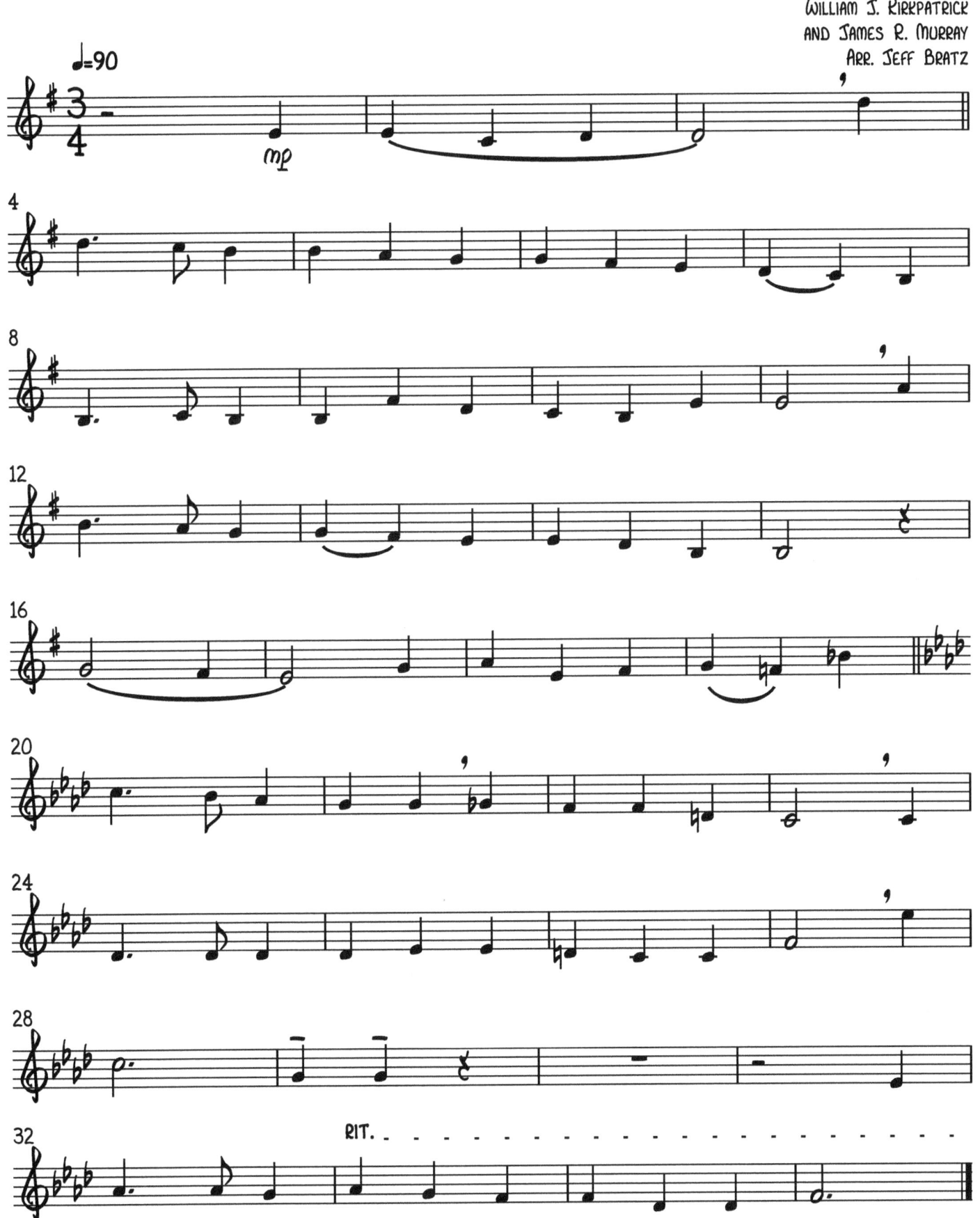

Additional
resources for
this arrangement

AIAM (SQ)
11-15-24

- 19 -

AIAM (SQ)
11-15-24

Additional resources for this arrangement

# AWAY IN A MANGER

Cello

William J. Kirkpatrick
and James R. Murray
Arr. Jeff Bratz

Additional resources for this arrangement

- 21 -

AIAM (SQ)
11-15-24

# DECK THE HALLS

Traditional Welsh Carol
Arr. Jeff Bratz

DTH (SQ)
11-17-24

# DECK THE HALLS

DTH (SQ)
11-17-24

# DECK THE HALLS

# DECK THE HALLS

DTH (SQ)
11-17-24

# DECK THE HALLS

DTH (SQ)
11-17-24

# DECK THE HALLS

Violin I

Traditional Welsh Carol
Arr. Jeff Bratz

DTH (SQ)
11-17-24

# DECK THE HALLS

# DECK THE HALLS

Violin II

Traditional Welsh Carol
Arr. Jeff Bratz
SWING

DTH (SQ)
11-17-24

# DECK THE HALLS

# DECK THE HALLS

Viola

Traditional Welsh Carol
Arr. Jeff Bratz

- 31 -

DTH (SQ)
11-17-24

# DECK THE HALLS

DTH (SQ)
11-17-24

# DECK THE HALLS

Cello

Traditional Welsh Carol
Arr. Jeff Bratz

DTH (SQ)
11-17-24

Cello
# DECK THE HALLS

DTH (SQ)
11-17-24

# THE FIRST NOEL

Traditional English Carol
Arr. Jeff Bratz

♩=80

TFN (SQ)
11-19-24

TFN (SQ)
11-19-24

TFN (SQ)
11-19-24

TFN (SQ)
11-19-24

Additional
resources for
this arrangement

# THE FIRST NOEL

Violin I

Traditional English Carol
Arr. Jeff Bratz

ISMN: 979-0-60026-085-0

Additional
resources for
this arrangement

- 39 -

TFN (SQ)
11-19-24

# THE FIRST NOEL

Violin II

Traditional English Carol
Arr. Jeff Bratz

TFN (SQ)
11-19-24

- 40 -

Additional resources for this arrangement

# THE FIRST NOEL

Viola

Traditional English Carol
Arr. Jeff Bratz

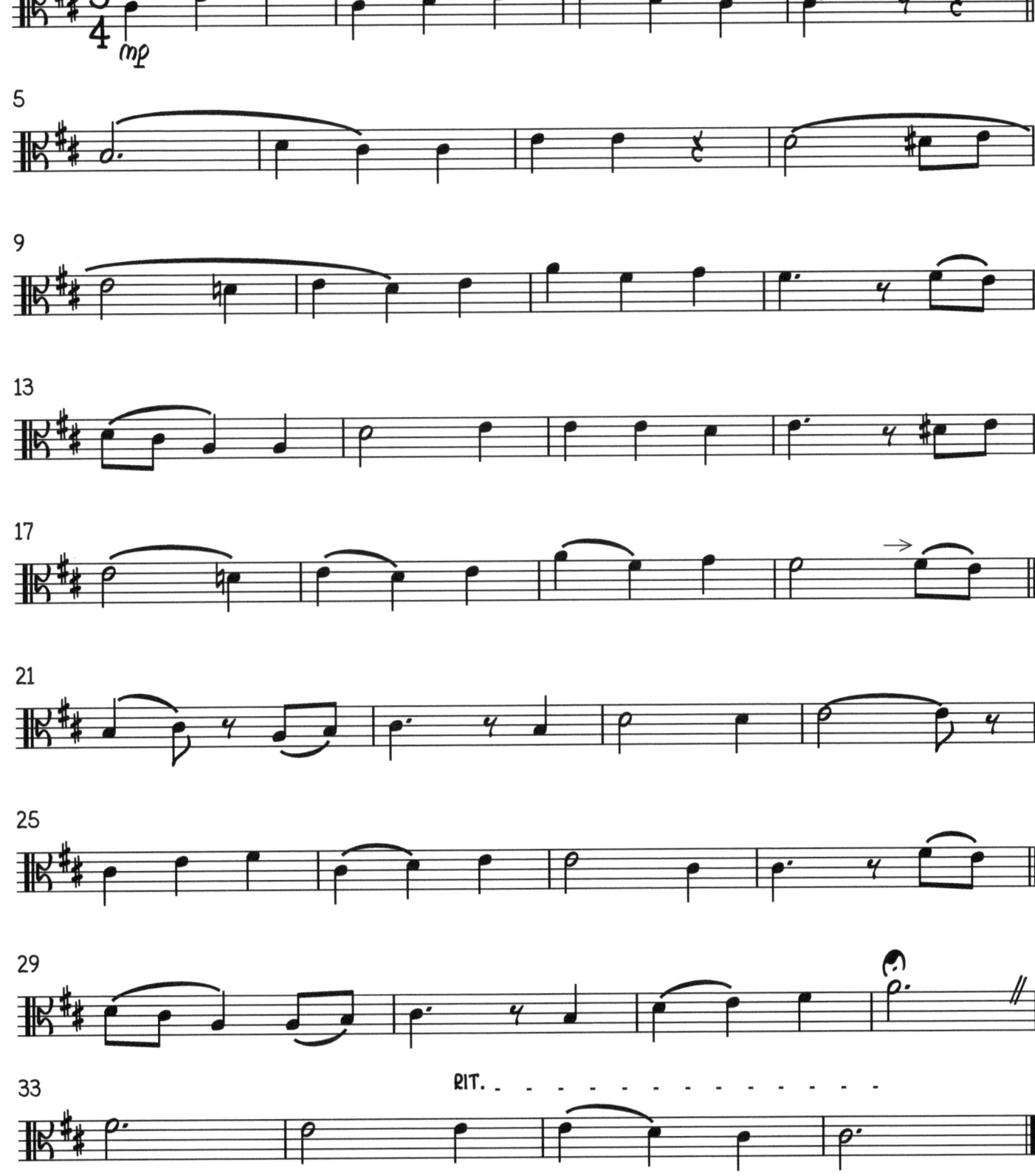

Additional resources for this arrangement

- 41 -

TFN (SQ)
11-19-24

# THE FIRST NOEL

Cello

TRADITIONAL ENGLISH CAROL
ARR. JEFF BRATZ

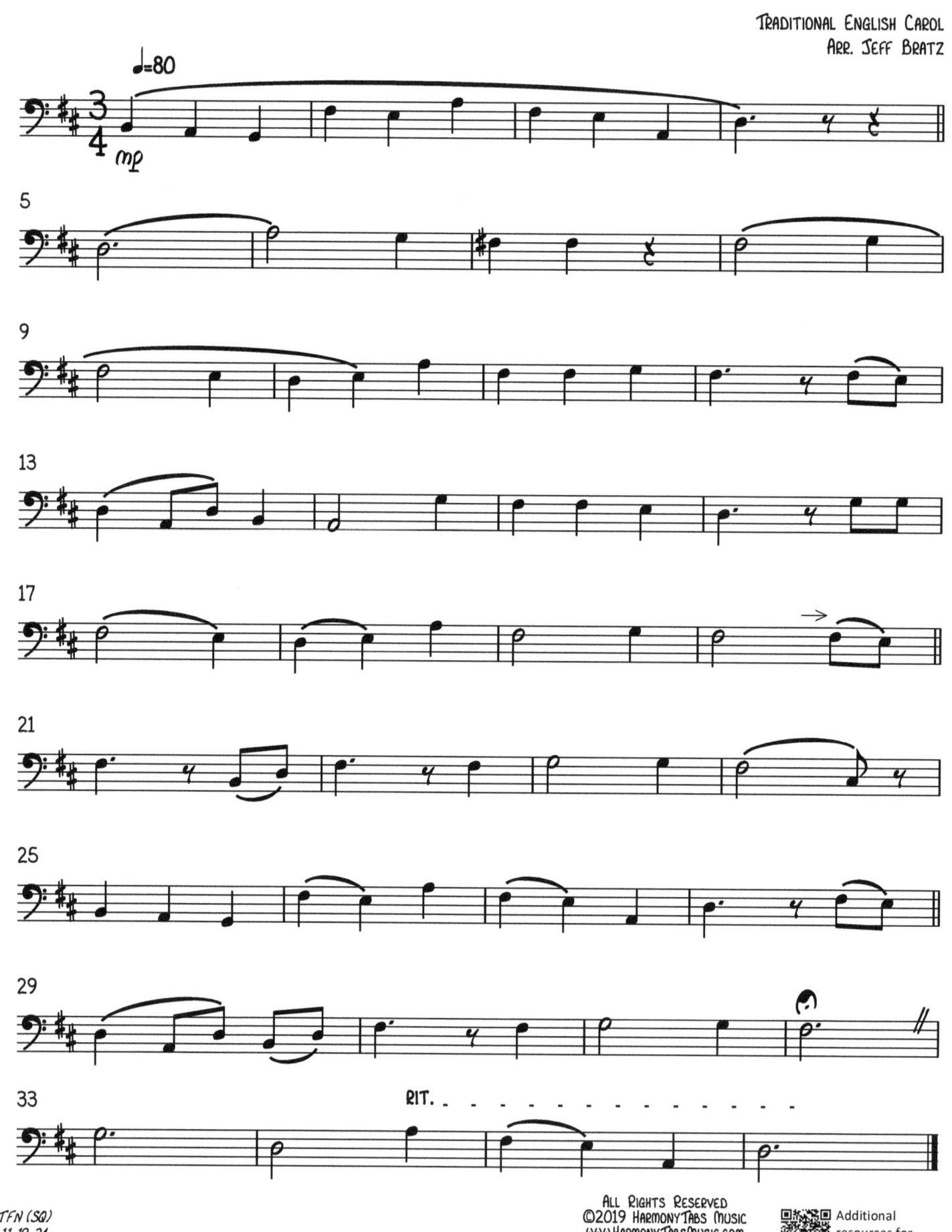

TFN (SQ)
11-19-24

- 42 -

Additional resources for this arrangement

# GO TELL IT ON THE MOUNTAIN

Compiled by
John Wesley Work, Jr.
Arr. Jeff Bratz

GT IOTM (SQ)
11-21-24

# GO TELL IT ON THE MOUNTAIN

GT1OTM (SQ)
11-21-24

Violin I

# GO TELL IT ON THE MOUNTAIN

Compiled by
John Wesley Work, Jr.
Arr. Jeff Bratz

♩=100 Swing

*mf*

TO CODA

D.S. al CODA

CODA

Additional resources for this arrangement

- 47 -

GT1OT(h) (SQ)
11-21-24

# GO TELL IT ON THE MOUNTAIN

Compiled by
John Wesley Work, Jr.
Arr. Jeff Bratz

GT Violin (SQ)
11-21-24

- 48 -

Additional resources for this arrangement

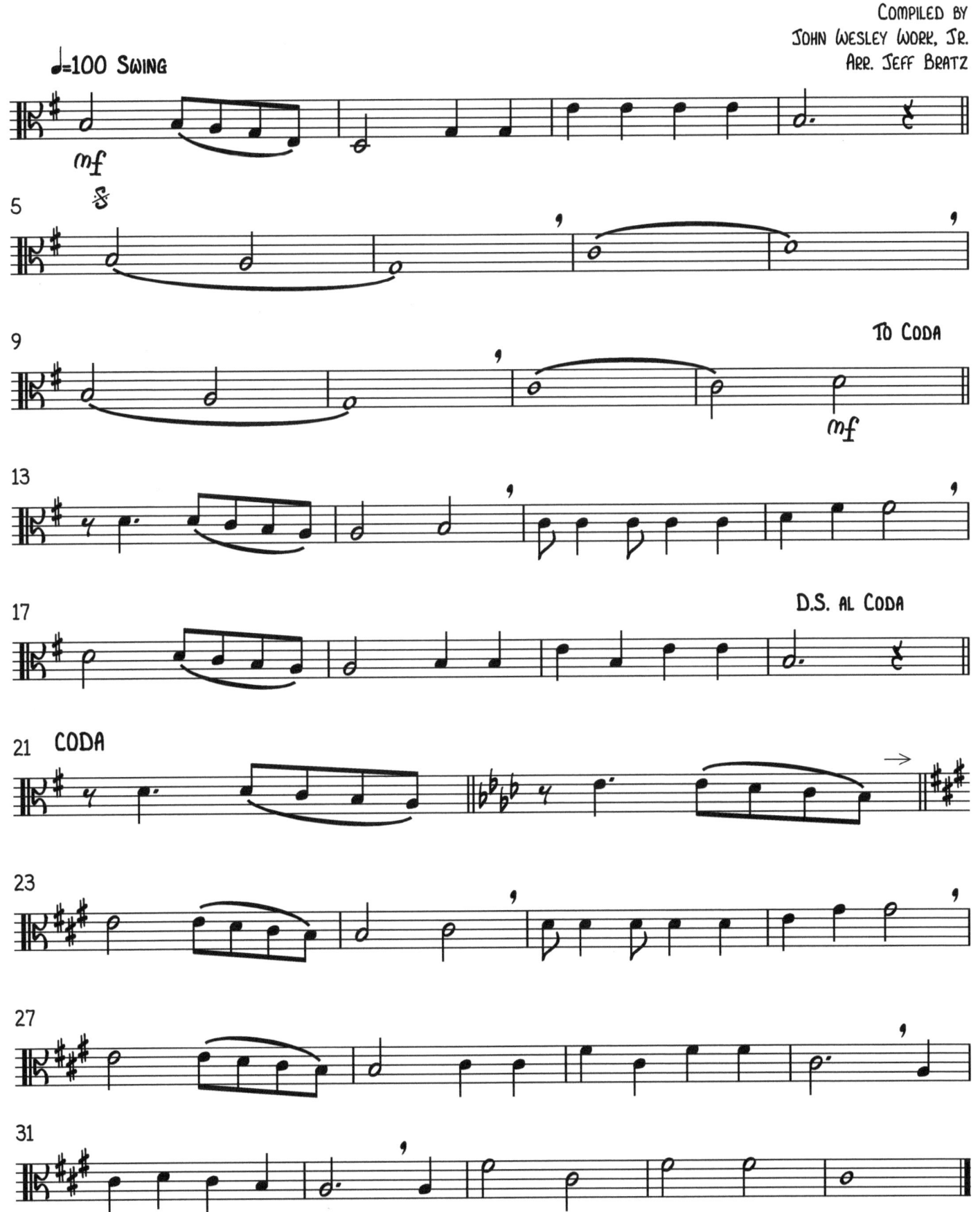

GT1DTM (SQ)
11-21-24

Additional resources for this arrangement

GT1DTM (SQ)
11-21-24

- 50 -

Additional
resources for
this arrangement

# GOD REST YE MERRY, GENTLEMEN

19th Century English Carol
Arr. Jeff Bratz

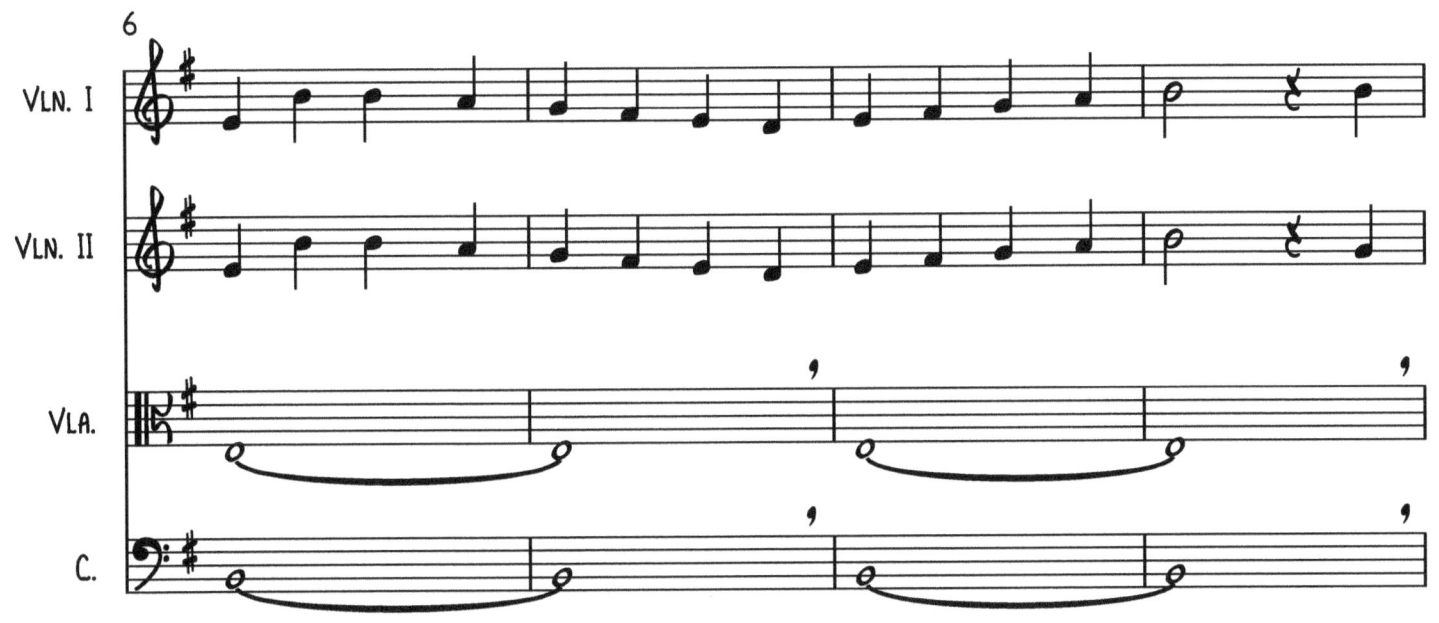

GRYMG (SQ)
11-22-24

# GOD REST YE MERRY, GENTLEMEN

GRY(MG (SQ)
11-22-24

GRYMG (SQ)
11-22-24

# GOD REST YE MERRY, GENTLEMEN

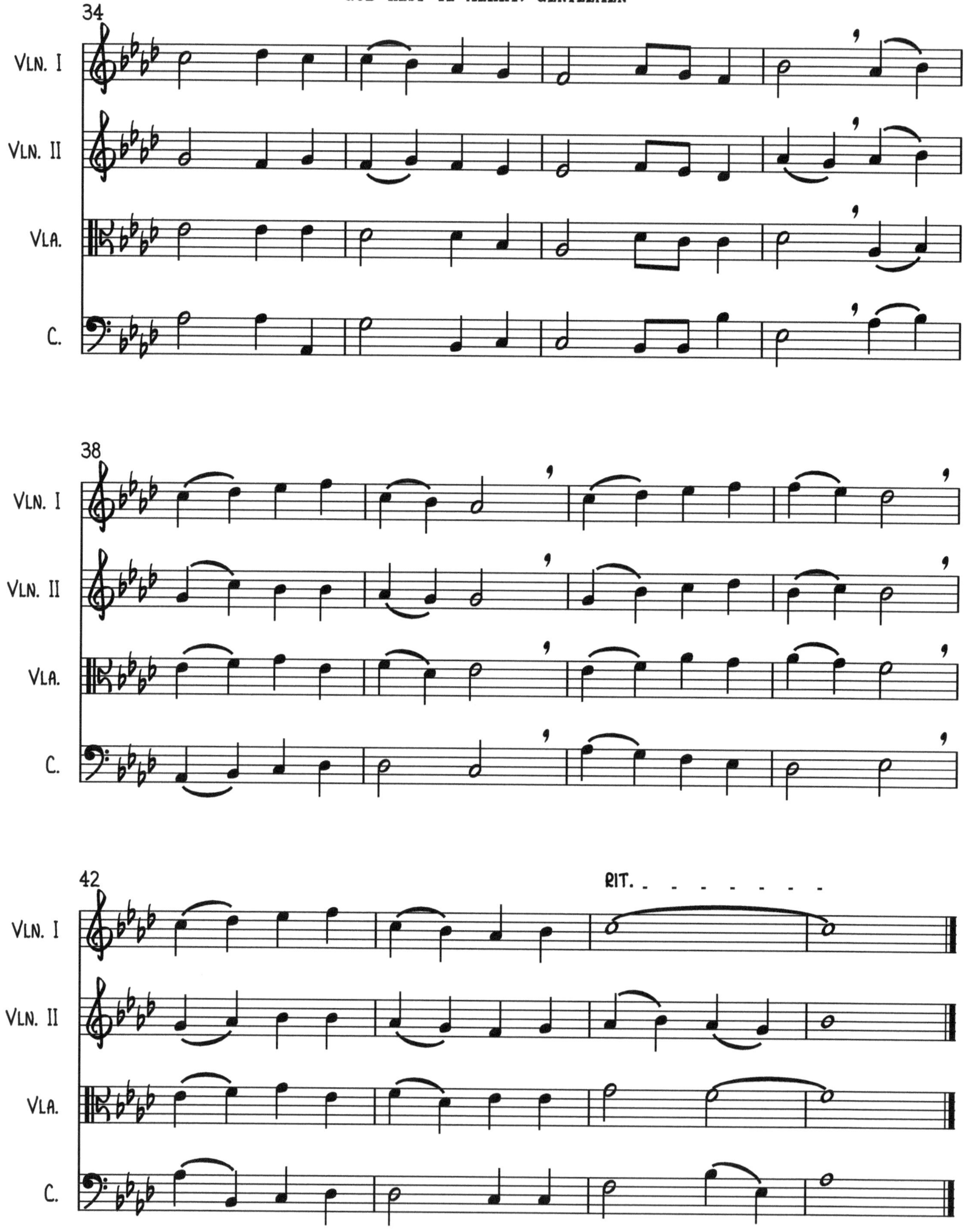

GRYMG (SQ)
11-22-24

# GOD REST YE MERRY, GENTLEMEN

Violin I

19th Century English Carol
Arr. Jeff Bratz

GRYMG (SQ)
11-22-24

# GOD REST YE MERRY, GENTLEMEN

GRYMG (SQ)
11-22-24

Additional resources for this arrangement

# GOD REST YE MERRY, GENTLEMEN

Violin II

19th Century English Carol
Arr. Jeff Bratz

GRYMG (SQ)
11-22-24

# GOD REST YE MERRY, GENTLEMEN

GRYMG (SQ)
11-22-24

# GOD REST YE MERRY, GENTLEMEN

Viola

19th Century English Carol
Arr. Jeff Bratz

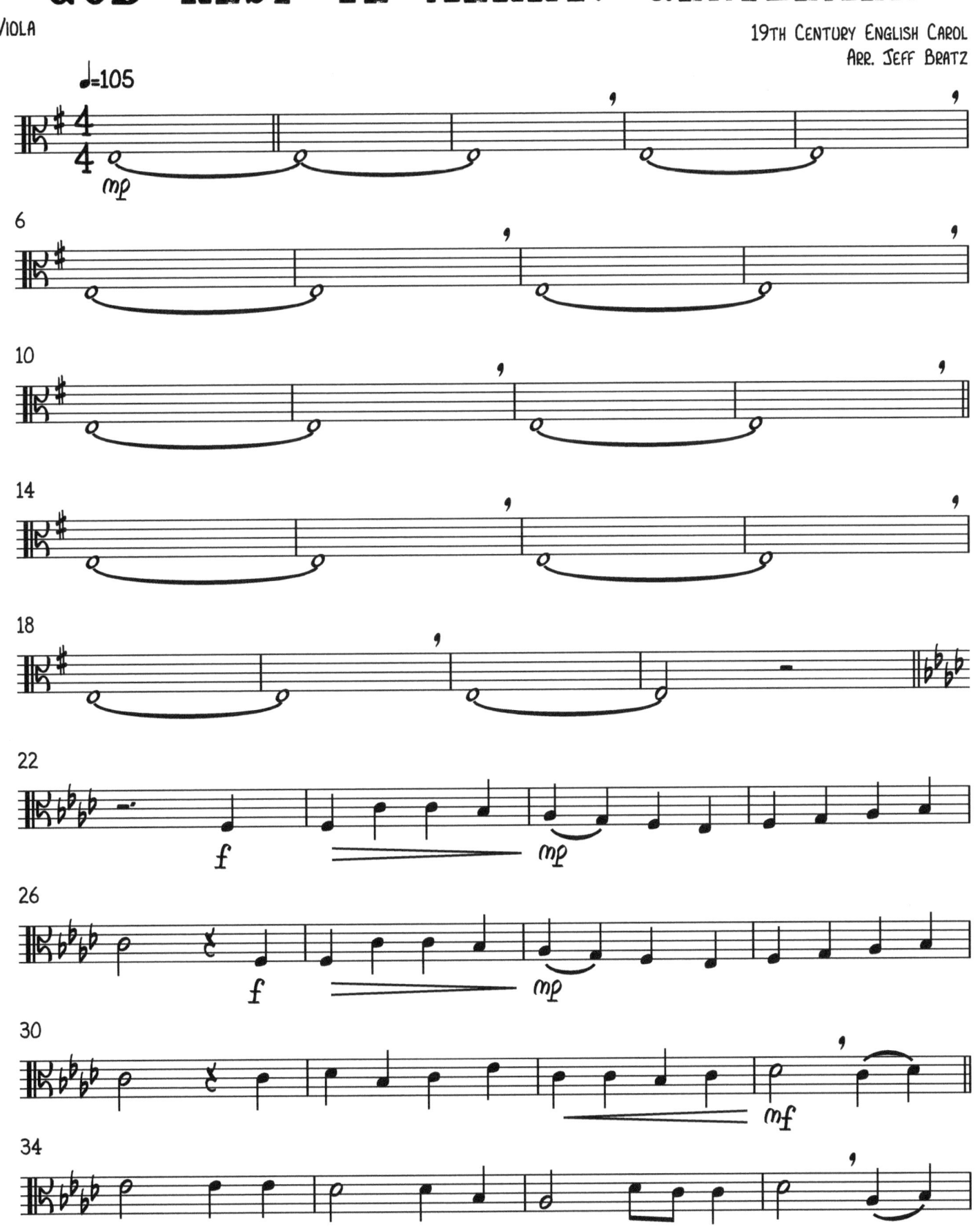

GRY MG (SQ)
11-22-24

# GOD REST YE MERRY, GENTLEMEN

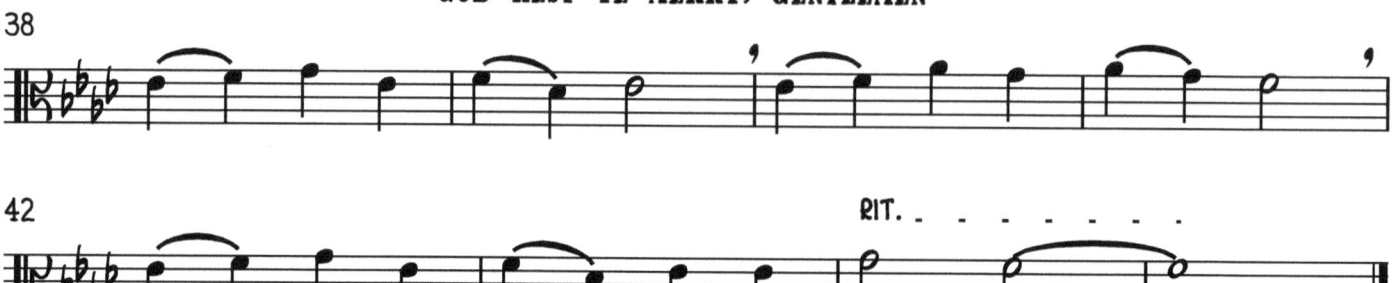

GRY(nG (SQ)
11-22-24

# GOD REST YE MERRY, GENTLEMEN

Cello

19th Century English Carol
Arr. Jeff Bratz

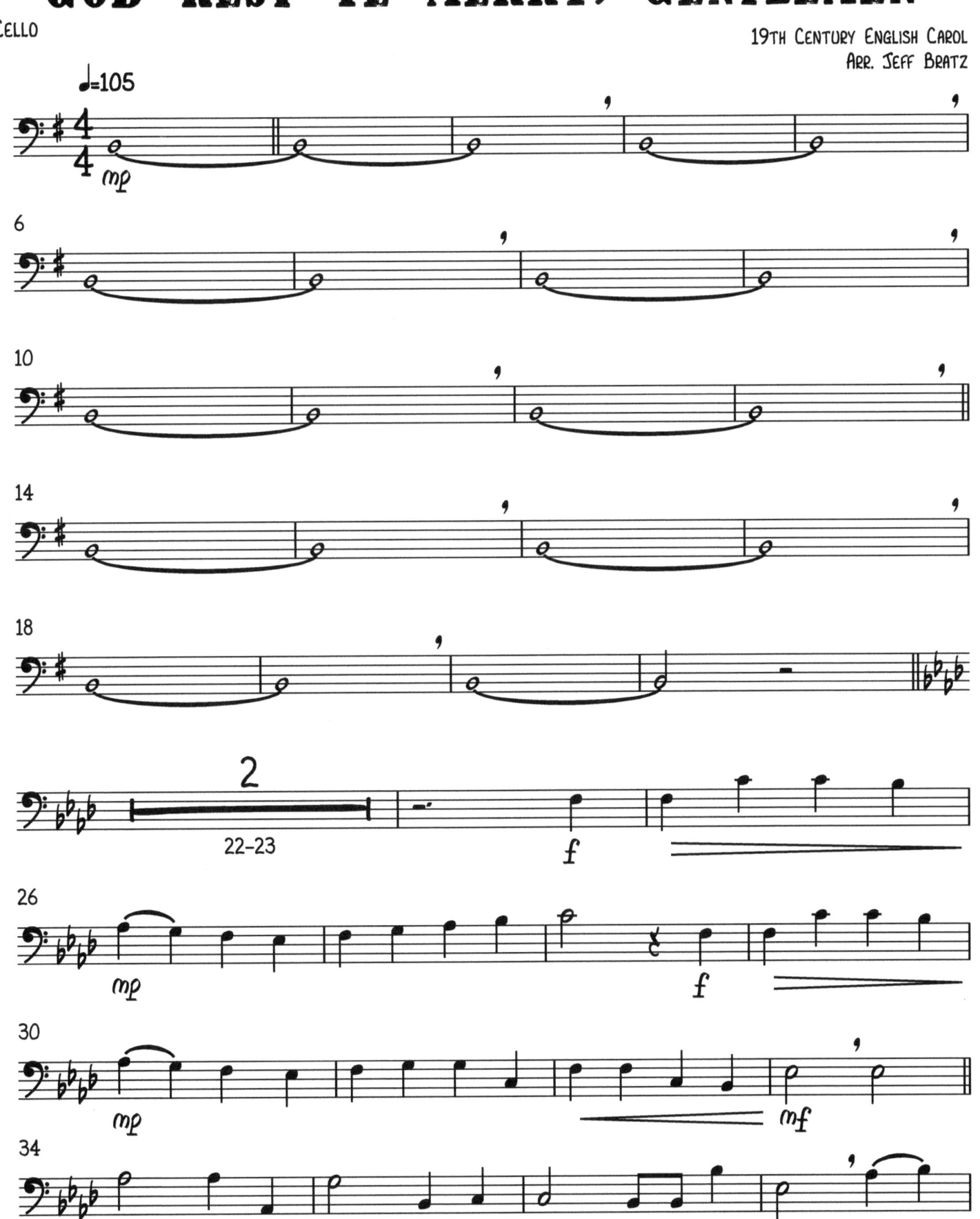

GRY/MG (SQ)
11-22-24

GRYmG (SQ)
11-22-24

# HALLELUJAH CHORUS
## (ABRIDGED)

George Friedrich Handel
arr. Jeff Bratz

HC (SQ)
12-5-24

# HALLELUJAH CHORUS (ABRIDGED)

HC (SQ)
12-5-24

# HALLELUJAH CHORUS (ABRIDGED)

HC (SQ)
12-5-24

# HALLELUJAH CHORUS
## (ABRIDGED)

George Friedrich Handel
arr. Jeff Bratz

HC (SQ)
12-5-24

Additional resources for this arrangement

# HALLELUJAH CHORUS
## (ABRIDGED)

Viola

George Friedrich Handel
arr. Jeff Bratz

Additional resources for this arrangement

HC (SQ)
12-5-24

Cello

# HALLELUJAH CHORUS
## (ABRIDGED)

George Friedrich Handel
Arr. Jeff Bratz

Additional
resources for
this arrangement

# HARK! THE HERALD ANGELS SING

Felix Mendelssohn
Lyrics by Charles Wesley
and George Whitefield
Arr. Jeff Bratz

HtHAS (SQ)
12-16-24

# HARK! THE HERALD ANGELS SING

HTHAS (SQ)
12-16-24

# HARK! THE HERALD ANGELS SING

HTHAS (SQ)
12-16-24

# HARK! THE HERALD ANGELS SING

Violin I

Felix Mendelssohn
Lyrics by Charles Wesley
and George Whitefield
Arr. Jeff Bratz

Additional
resources for
this arrangement

- 75 -

HTHAS (SQ)
12-16-24

# HARK! THE HERALD ANGELS SING

Violin II

Felix Mendelssohn
Lyrics by Charles Wesley
and George Whitefield
Arr. Jeff Bratz

HTHAS (SQ)
12-16-24

Additional
resources for
this arrangement

# HARK! THE HERALD ANGELS SING

Viola

Felix Mendelssohn
Lyrics by Charles Wesley
and George Whitefield
Arr. Jeff Bratz

HTHAS (SQ)
12-16-24

- 77 -

# HARK! THE HERALD ANGELS SING

Cello

Felix Mendelssohn
Lyrics by Charles Wesley
and George Whitefield
Arr. Jeff Bratz

# I SAW THREE SHIPS

Traditional
Arr. Jeff Bratz

ISTS (SQ)
12-17-24

# I SAW THREE SHIPS

# I SAW THREE SHIPS

ISTS (SQ)
12-17-24

ISTS (SQ)
12-17-24

# I SAW THREE SHIPS

Violin I

Traditional
Arr. Jeff Bratz

ISTS (SQ)
12-17-24

- 84 -

# I SAW THREE SHIPS

*ISTS (SQ)*
*12-17-24*

# I SAW THREE SHIPS

Traditional
Arr. Jeff Bratz

ISTS (SQ)
12-17-24
ISMN: 979-0-60026-084-3

# I SAW THREE SHIPS

ISTS (SQ)
12-17-24

# I SAW THREE SHIPS

Viola

Traditional
Arr. Jeff Bratz

ISTS (SQ)
12-17-24

VIOLA
# I SAW THREE SHIPS

ISTS (SQ)
12-17-24

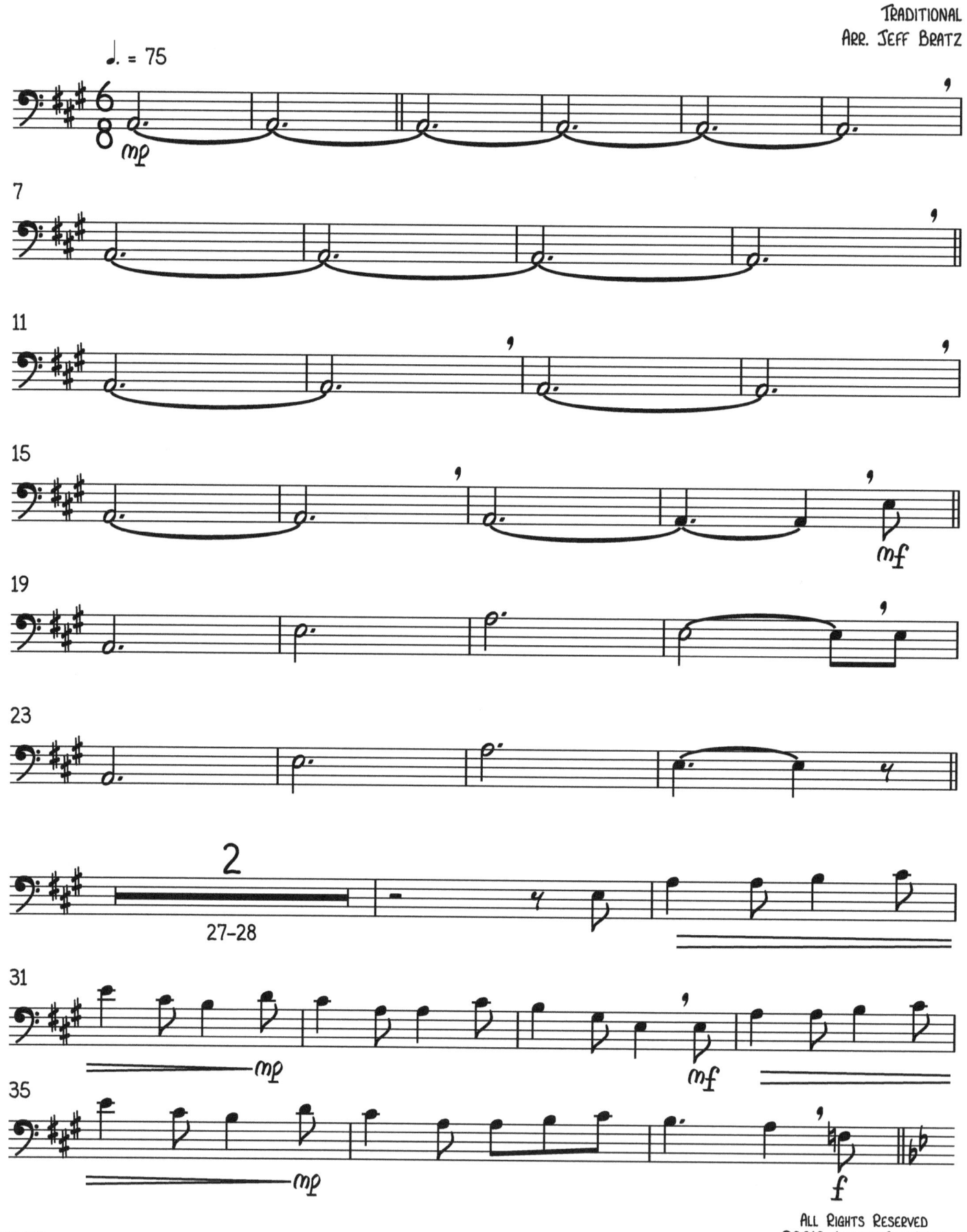

ISTS (SQ)
12-17-24

# I SAW THREE SHIPS

ISTS (SQ)
12-17-24

# FINAL WORDS

Please consider leaving a review of this book. I would greatly appreciate it. It will help me to continue on this book writing journey I've set off on.

Thank you in advance!

## LEAVE A REVIEW

## HARMONYTABS EMAIL LIST

Once again, here is the link to the HarmonyTabs email list to keep you up to speed on any new music, publications, and promotions.

## ABOUT THE AUTHOR

Jeff Bratz has a degree in Professional Music from the School for Music Vocations and a Professional Certificate in Music Theory and Composition from Berklee College of Music. He's a composer and arranger specializing in vocal arrangements. In a former life, Jeff was a music teacher for grades pre-k through high school. He has sung in dozens of vocal groups including The Dickens Carolers at Disneyland's *Club 33*, The Fault Line on *America's Got Talent*, and Manhattan Transfer tribute group LA Transfer. He was also part of the Downbeat award-winning First Take. He currently performs with rock band RaDIUM, 80s rock tribute band 8IGHTY 6IXX, and salsa band Calle Mambo. He lives in Massachusetts with his wonderful partner Kristen and the cutest nugget that ever nuggeted: Ollie!

# Also Available From

# HarmonyTabs

## Sheet Music

-A Cappella Choirs/Groups
-Brass Ensembles
-String Ensembles
-Sax Ensembles
And More!

HARMONYTABS.COM/SHEET-MUSIC/

## Songbooks

-Wind Ensembles
-A Cappella Choirs/Groups
-Flute Ensembles
-Brass Ensembles
And More!

HARMONYTABS.COM/MUSIC-BOOKS/SONGBOOKS/

## Music Theory and Instruction

-An Incomplete Crash Course
in Contemporary Music Theory:
The Fundamentals

More to Come!

HARMONYTABS.COM/MUSIC-BOOKS/INSTRUCTIONAL-BOOKS/

## Music Composition

-Standard Manuscript Notebook
-Pocket Manuscript Notebook
-Writing Prompt Journals

More to Come!

HARMONYTABS.COM/MUSIC-BOOKS/MUSIC-COMPOSITION-BOOKS/

HarmonyTabsMusic.com

www.ingramcontent.com/pod-product-compliance
Lightning Source LLC
Chambersburg PA
CBHW041121120626

46547CB00019B/2798